DASHER GOES FOR A WALK

Dave Martellaro

Dedication

I dedicate this book to my very good friend, wife, and significant other, Bonnie. Bonnie, provided me the motivation and ideas to continue the life and adventures of Dasher. Her almost daily interactions and walks with Loki provide further adventures for me to write about for children to enjoy and parents to read to. Bonnie joined me with Angel, her Chihuahua, who also brings excitement and fun with Loki. This book brings forward excitement and awareness that a Spring Walk can bring. Loki and Angel enjoy standing up against a tree watching the squirrels looking down at them, smelling the new smells of Spring, and the different flowers that they go and smell.

Much like a child holding their parent's hand as mom or dad point out and describe the new surroundings to them.

About the Author

I was born in South Bend, Indiana, where I spent my childhood and much of my teenage years. I attended Northern Illinois University and have been in IT for what seems like all my life. I have always enjoyed telling stories, whether from books or making them up for children to engage their imaginations. My intention in writing these stories about Dasher's exploits was to capture and highlight important life lessons to help children deal with everyday life. Also, as a parent, I enjoyed sitting with my children and reading to them, as I hope this will also draw parents into reading to their children. When not working or writing, I enjoy watching college football and movies with Dashers' inspiration, my dog Loki.

In a cozy home, Dasher, a bouncy Springer Spaniel pup, lived with his dad, Ben and with a happy family consisting of Mother, Father, Suzi, and Jimmy. Suzi and Jimmy were Dasher's play buddies, while Father and Ben went on fun adventures together. Mother made sure Dasher and Ben had yummy food and warm beds.

TOYS

Normally Dasher would spend the day playing with Suzi and Jimmy, sitting and talking to Ben, his dad, playing with his toys or napping the day away. But his favorite thing to do was going for a walk. Sometimes Mother took him for his walks, or Father took him and Ben at the same time, but most of the time he went walking with Suzi.

Lately though his walk had been short and it had been very cold outside. Dasher and Suzi would walk through areas covered with something white and wet. Dashers dad, Ben, explained to him 'Son, I have heard that it is called snow and it comes once a year'. Dasher asked,' How long does it stay and does it ever get warm again? I am so tired of staying in so much and doing nothing'. 'Yes Dasher, it does get warm and the snow goes away' said Ben.

After that Dasher would spend his day looking out the window to see if the snow was going away. One day, while standing on the couch looking out through the window, he saw a lot of the snow gone and warm sunlight coming through the window. Dasher got excited and jumped off the couch and ran to Suzi. He was very excited and wanted to go see what it was like outside.

Suzi guessed that Dasher wanted to go for a walk, so she put on a jacket and put Dasher's leash on him and they walked out the door. The first thing Dasher noticed was that it was not as cold as the other days and the sun felt nice and warm as it shined down on Suzi and him. He felt bouncy and alive walking outside on this beautiful day.

10

As they walked down the sidewalk, Dasher heard the sounds of birds chirping away. He had not heard these sounds for a long time. He looked around and saw many colorful birds in the trees and flying around the sky. Up in the trees he saw birds with twigs and other things making nests. The sky was so blue and clear and the air was refreshing. What a wonderful day for a walk he thought.

As they continued their walk, Suzi took Dasher into a park. Ahead of him were two squirrels running around after each other and playing. Sometimes they would stop and pick up acorns from the ground. When the squirrels saw Suzi and Dasher they ran to a nearby tree and climbed up to a branch and stared down at Dasher. Dasher looked up and he saw some things of different colors appearing on many of the limbs. Ben would later tell him that the tree was making new leaves.

14

Dasher and Suzi walked further into the park and Dasher heard other children laughing and screaming. He remembered that when it was cold there were no children in the park. The children were playing on many of the swings. He also saw other dogs walking with other people. This made him feel that Suzi may be taking him for more walks since the days were nice and many people were out enjoying themselves. He would be able to meet and play with other dogs he had met before.

16

As Suzi and Dasher were returning home Dasher saw something that surprised him as they walked up the sidewalk to the door. Dasher could see green stems growing out of Mother's garden. He remembered last year all the pretty flowers that she had planted there. He wondered if they were growing again and he couldn't wait to see what would happen to them. He was so happy Suzi had taken him for a walk. There was so much to see and would there be more new things he didn't see today? He was anxious to find out tomorrow.

As Dasher and Suzi entered the house they heard Mother call out 'Did you two have a nice walk?'. 'Yes Mother', answered Suzi,' it was wonderful. So much better than all that snow and cold' answered Suzi. Ben walked up to Dasher and asked 'Did you have a good time, son?'. Dasher told his dad of all the things he saw and how exciting it was to see that the days were returning to how they were before the snow. He couldn't wait to go out tomorrow to see new things.

Dasher realized that with the days getting warmer and the snow going away, he would make sure to go with Suzi or Mother on his walks, Being outside would bring new things to see and do. He looked forward to going for more walks and especially with his dad, Ben. When he went with his dad, Ben would point out things of interest and things Dasher never realized before. In the years ahead Dasher would warmly remember the walks with Suzi, Mother, and especially with Ben. Walking with his dad and spending that time with him gave Dasher wonderful memories that he would fall asleep to when he was older.

The end